Weird Cookies:

Strange and Unusual Cookies for the Adventurous Baker

100 RECIPES THAT WILL HAVE PEOPLE TALKING

By Robert Griffith

www.askgriff.com

ISBN: 9798390813911

Printed in the United States of America

First Edition

TABLE OF CONTENTS

INTRODUCTION: **Error! Bookmark not defined.**

IT HAS WHAT IN IT!? 8

Blackberry Lavender Cookies 9

Carrot and Ginger Cookies 10

Lavender and Honey Cookies 11

Gorgonzola and Walnut Cookies 12

Sweet Potato Pie Cookies 13

Cornmeal and Honey Cookies 14

Rosemary Olive Oil Cookies 15

Blue Cheese and Fig Cookies 16

Black Sesame Cookies 17

Bacon Chocolate Chip Cookies 18

Salted Caramel Pretzel Cookies 19

Lavender Shortbread Cookies 20

Matcha Green Tea Cookies 21

Lavender Honey Cookies 22

Red Bean Paste Cookies 23

Avocado Cookies 24

Black Licorice Cookies 25

Matcha White Chocolate Cookies 26

Rosewater Shortbread Cookies 27

Cornflake Cookies 28

Sweet Potato Cookies 29

Oatmeal Raisin Cookies with Bacon 30

Peanut Butter and Jelly Cookies 31

Mango Lassi Cookies 32

Lemon and Lavender Cookies 33

Sweet Potato and Marshmallow Cookies 34

Rosewater Almond Cookies 35

Saffron Cardamom Cookies 36

SPICING THINGS UP 37

Spicy Cheddar Cookies 38

Spicy Chocolate Chipotle Cookies 39

Spicy Mexican Hot Chocolate Cookies 40

Spicy Ancho Chili and Dark Chocolate Cookies 40

Spicy Harissa and Cheddar Cookies 42

Spicy Chili Chocolate Cookies 43

Spicy Cumin and Coriander Cookies 44

Spicy Cardamom and Black Pepper Cookies 45

Miso Sesame Cookies 46

Spicy Szechuan Peppercorn and Cherry Cookies 47

Miso Butter Cookies 48

Spicy Gingerbread Cookies 48

Chili Chocolate Cookies 50

Miso Caramel Cookies 51

Curry Cookies 52

Wasabi Pea Cookies 53

Wasabi Pea and Pickle Cookies 54

Wasabi Ginger Cookies 55

Curry Coconut Cookies 55

Chili Chocolate and Bacon Cookies 57

CAFFEINE COMMITMENT 58

Mocha Cookies 59

Espresso and Dark Chocolate Cookies 59

Coffee and Cardamom Cookies 60

Cold Brew and Coconut Cookies 61

Caramel Macchiato Cookies 62

French Press and Maple Cookies 63

Coffee and Caramel Cookies 65
Vietnamese Iced Coffee Cookies 66
Coffee and Toffee Cookies 67
Coffee and Gingerbread Cookies 68
Coffee and Nutella Cookies 69
Coffee and Vanilla Bean Cookies 70
TREATS FROM THE GROWN-UPS TABLE 71
Whiskey Pecan Cookies 72
Beer Cookies 73
Bourbon and Maple Cookies 74
Red Wine Chocolate Cookies 75
Beer and Pretzel Cookies 76
Tequila Sunrise Cookies 76
Margarita Cookies 78
Irish Whiskey and Baileys Cookies 79
White Russian Cookies 79
Rum and Raisin Cookies 80
Kahlua and Mocha Cookies 81
Prosecco and Strawberry Cookies 82
Gin and Tonic Cookies 84
Cointreau and Orange Cookies 85
Amaretto and Almond Cookies 86
CREATIVE ICING IDEAS **Error! Bookmark not defined.**
Coffee Icing 87
Maple Bacon Icing 88
Wasabi Icing 88
Red Pepper Flake Icing 89
Garlic Icing 89
Peanut Butter and Jelly Icing 89
Honey Mustard Icing 90

Gingerbread Latte Icing 90
Lavender Honey Icing 90
Blue Cheese and Pear Icing 91
Spicy Chocolate Icing 91
Honey Sriracha Icing 91
Maple Syrup and Bacon Icing 92
Pickle Juice Icing 92
Curry Icing 92
CONCLUSION 93

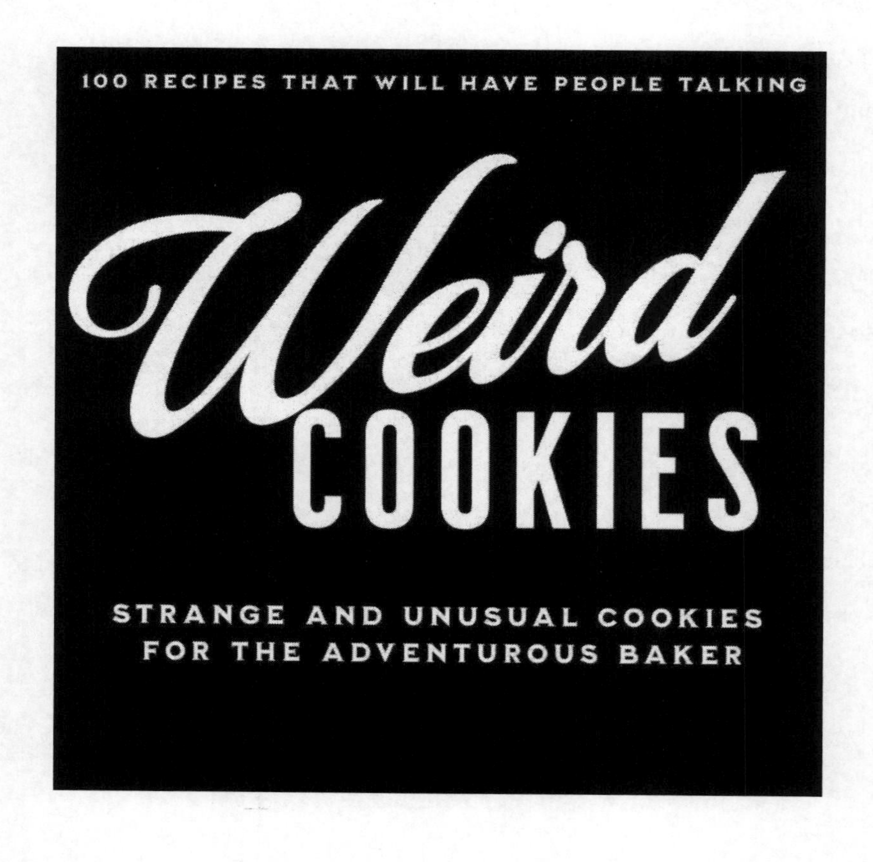

INTRODUCTION:

Welcome to the world of unusual cookie recipes! In this book, you'll find a collection of tasty treats that are sure to surprise and delight your taste buds. From the bold and spicy flavors of chili chocolate and wasabi pea cookies, to the unique and unexpected ingredients like avocado and sweet potato, these recipes are sure to satisfy your cravings for something different. We've even thrown in a section of flavors more attuned to the adult palate with ingredients such as bourbon, whiskey, beer, and wine.

But these cookies are not just for the adventurous foodie – they're also perfect for the home baker looking to try something new. Whether you're an experienced baker or a beginner, these recipes are easy to follow and fun to make. So put on your apron, preheat your oven, and get ready to explore the delicious world of unusual cookie recipes!

Be forewarned, these flavor combinations obviously won't appeal to everyone, but that's part of the fun in discovering something new.

IT HAS WHAT IN IT!?

Cookies With Exotic and Unusual Flavors

Blackberry Lavender Cookies

Ingredients:

- 1 cup unsalted butter, softened
- 1 cup sugar
- 2 large eggs
- 1 tsp lavender extract
- 2 cups all-purpose flour
- 1 tsp baking powder
- 1 tsp salt
- 1 cup blackberries
- 1 cup white chocolate chips

Instructions:

1. Preheat your oven to 350°F (175°C) and line a baking sheet with parchment paper.
2. In a large mixing bowl, beat together the butter and sugar until well combined.
3. Beat in the eggs, followed by the lavender extract.
4. In a separate bowl, whisk together the flour, baking powder, and salt.
5. Gradually add the dry mixture to the butter mixture and mix until well combined.
6. Stir in the blackberries and white chocolate chips.
7. Drop rounded spoonfuls of dough onto the prepared baking sheet.
8. Bake for 10-12 minutes, or until the edges are lightly golden.
9. Allow the cookies to cool on the baking sheet for a few minutes before transferring to a wire rack to cool completely.

Carrot and Ginger Cookies

Ingredients:

- 1 cup unsalted butter, softened
- 1 cup sugar
- 2 large eggs
- 1 cup grated carrots
- 2 tbsp finely minced ginger
- 2 cups all-purpose flour
- 1 tsp baking powder
- 1 tsp salt
- 1 cup chopped walnuts

Instructions:

1. Preheat your oven to 350°F (175°C) and line a baking sheet with parchment paper.
2. In a large mixing bowl, beat together the butter and sugar until well combined.
3. Beat in the eggs.
4. In a separate bowl, whisk together the flour, baking powder, and salt.
5. Gradually add the dry mixture to the butter mixture and mix until well combined.
6. Stir in the grated carrots, minced ginger, and chopped walnuts.
7. Drop rounded spoonfuls of dough onto the prepared baking sheet.
8. Bake for 10-12 minutes, or until the edges are lightly golden.
9. Allow the cookies to cool on the baking sheet for a few minutes before transferring to a wire rack to cool completely.

Lavender and Honey Cookies

Ingredients:

- 1 cup unsalted butter, softened
- 1 cup honey
- 2 large eggs
- 1 tsp lavender extract
- 2 cups all-purpose flour
- 1 cup rolled oats
- 1 tsp baking powder
- 1 tsp salt
- 1/2 cup dried lavender

Instructions:

1. Preheat your oven to 350°F (175°C) and line a baking sheet with parchment paper.
2. In a large mixing bowl, beat together the butter and honey until well combined.
3. Beat in the eggs, followed by the lavender extract.
4. In a separate bowl, whisk together the flour, oats, baking powder, and salt.
5. Gradually add the dry mixture to the butter mixture and mix until well combined.
6. Stir in the dried lavender.
7. Drop rounded spoonfuls of dough onto the prepared baking sheet.
8. Bake for 10-12 minutes, or until the edges are lightly golden.
9. Allow the cookies to cool on the baking sheet for a few minutes before transferring to a wire rack to cool completely.

Gorgonzola and Walnut Cookies

Ingredients:

- 1 cup unsalted butter, softened
- 1 cup crumbled gorgonzola cheese
- 1 cup sugar
- 2 large eggs
- 2 1/4 cups all-purpose flour
- 1 tsp baking powder
- 1 tsp salt
- 1 cup chopped walnuts

Instructions:

1. Preheat your oven to 350°F (175°C) and line a baking sheet with parchment paper.
2. In a large mixing bowl, beat together the butter, gorgonzola cheese, and sugar until well combined.
3. Beat in the eggs.
4. In a separate bowl, whisk together the flour, baking powder, and salt.
5. Gradually add the dry mixture to the butter mixture and mix until well combined.
6. Stir in the chopped walnuts.
7. Drop rounded spoonfuls of dough onto the prepared baking sheet.
8. Bake for 10-12 minutes, or until the edges are lightly golden.
9. Allow the cookies to cool on the baking sheet for a few minutes before transferring to a wire rack to cool completely.

Sweet Potato Pie Cookies

Ingredients:

- 1 cup unsalted butter, softened
- 1 cup packed brown sugar
- 2 large eggs
- 1 cup mashed sweet potatoes
- 1 tsp vanilla extract
- 2 cups all-purpose flour
- 1 tsp baking powder
- 1 tsp salt
- 1 tsp cinnamon
- 1/2 tsp nutmeg
- 1/4 tsp allspice
- 1 cup chopped pecans
- 1 cup raisins

Instructions:

1. Preheat your oven to 350°F (175°C) and line a baking sheet with parchment paper.
2. In a large mixing bowl, beat together the butter and brown sugar until well combined.
3. Beat in the eggs, followed by the mashed sweet potatoes and vanilla extract.
4. In a separate bowl, whisk together the flour, baking powder, salt, cinnamon, nutmeg, and allspice.
5. Gradually add the dry mixture to the butter mixture and mix until well combined.
6. Stir in the chopped pecans and raisins.
7. Drop rounded spoonfuls of dough onto the prepared baking sheet.
8. Bake for 10-12 minutes, or until the edges are lightly golden.
9. Allow the cookies to cool on the baking sheet for a few minutes before transferring to a wire rack to cool completely.

Cornmeal and Honey Cookies

Ingredients:

- 1 cup unsalted butter, softened
- 1 cup honey
- 2 large eggs
- 2 cups all-purpose flour
- 1 cup cornmeal
- 1 tsp baking powder
- 1 tsp salt

Instructions:

1. Preheat your oven to 350°F (175°C) and line a baking sheet with parchment paper.
2. In a large mixing bowl, beat together the butter and honey until well combined.
3. Beat in the eggs.
4. In a separate bowl, whisk together the flour, cornmeal, baking powder, and salt.
5. Gradually add the dry mixture to the butter mixture and mix until well combined.
6. Drop rounded spoonfuls of dough onto the prepared baking sheet.
7. Bake for 10-12 minutes, or until the edges are lightly golden.
8. Allow the cookies to cool on the baking sheet for a few minutes before transferring to a wire rack to cool completely.

Rosemary Olive Oil Cookies

Ingredients:

- 1 cup olive oil
- 1 cup sugar
- 2 large eggs
- 2 tsp vanilla extract
- 2 cups all-purpose flour
- 1 tsp baking powder
- 1 tsp salt
- 2 tbsp fresh rosemary, finely chopped

Instructions:

1. Preheat your oven to 350°F (175°C) and line a baking sheet with parchment paper.
2. In a large mixing bowl, beat together the olive oil and sugar until well combined.
3. Beat in the eggs, one at a time, followed by the vanilla extract.
4. In a separate bowl, whisk together the flour, baking powder, and salt.
5. Gradually add the dry mixture to the oil mixture and mix until well combined.
6. Stir in the chopped rosemary.
7. Drop rounded spoonfuls of dough onto the prepared baking sheet.
8. Bake for 10-12 minutes, or until the edges are lightly golden.
9. Allow the cookies to cool on the baking sheet for a few minutes before transferring to a wire rack to cool completely.

Blue Cheese and Fig Cookies

Ingredients:

- 1 cup unsalted butter, softened
- 1 cup crumbled blue cheese
- 1 cup brown sugar
- 1/2 cup granulated sugar
- 2 large eggs
- 1 tsp vanilla extract
- 2 1/4 cups all-purpose flour
- 1 tsp baking soda
- 1 tsp salt
- 1 cup dried figs, chopped

Instructions:

1. Preheat your oven to 350°F (175°C) and line a baking sheet with parchment paper.
2. In a large mixing bowl, cream together the butter, blue cheese, and sugars until smooth.
3. Beat in the eggs, one at a time, followed by the vanilla extract.
4. In a separate bowl, whisk together the flour, baking soda, and salt.
5. Gradually add the dry mixture to the butter mixture and mix until well combined.
6. Stir in the chopped figs.
7. Drop rounded spoonfuls of dough onto the prepared baking sheet.
8. Bake for 10-12 minutes, or until the edges are lightly golden.
9. Allow the cookies to cool on the baking sheet for a few minutes before transferring to a wire rack to cool completely.

Black Sesame Cookies

Ingredients:

- 1 cup unsalted butter, softened
- 1 cup sugar
- 2 large eggs
- 2 tsp black sesame paste
- 2 1/4 cups all-purpose flour
- 1 tsp baking soda
- 1 tsp salt
- 1/2 cup black sesame seeds

Instructions:

1. Preheat your oven to 350°F (175°C) and line a baking sheet with parchment paper.
2. In a large mixing bowl, cream together the butter and sugar until smooth.
3. Beat in the eggs, one at a time, followed by the black sesame paste.
4. In a separate bowl, whisk together the flour, baking soda, and salt.
5. Gradually add the dry mixture to the butter mixture and mix until well combined.
6. Stir in the black sesame seeds.
7. Drop rounded spoonfuls of dough onto the prepared baking sheet.
8. Bake for 10-12 minutes, or until the edges are lightly golden.
9. Allow the cookies to cool on the baking sheet for a few minutes before transferring to a wire rack to cool completely.

Bacon Chocolate Chip Cookies

Ingredients:

- 1/2 cup unsalted butter, softened
- 1/2 cup bacon grease, melted
- 1 cup brown sugar
- 1/2 cup granulated sugar
- 2 large eggs
- 1 tsp vanilla extract
- 2 1/4 cups all-purpose flour
- 1 tsp baking soda
- 1 tsp salt
- 1 cup semisweet chocolate chips
- 1/2 cup bacon bits

Instructions:

1. Preheat your oven to 350°F (175°C) and line a baking sheet with parchment paper.
2. In a large mixing bowl, cream together the butter and bacon grease until smooth.
3. Beat in the sugars, eggs, and vanilla extract.
4. In a separate bowl, whisk together the flour, baking soda, and salt.
5. Gradually add the dry mixture to the butter mixture and mix until well combined.
6. 6. Stir in the chocolate chips and bacon bits.
7. Drop rounded spoonfuls of dough onto the prepared baking sheet.
8. Bake for 10-12 minutes, or until the edges are lightly golden.
9. Allow the cookies to cool on the baking sheet for a few minutes before transferring to a wire rack to cool completely.

Salted Caramel Pretzel Cookies

Ingredients:

- 1 cup unsalted butter, softened
- 1 cup brown sugar
- 1/2 cup granulated sugar
- 2 large eggs
- 1 tsp vanilla extract
- 2 1/4 cups all-purpose flour
- 1 tsp baking soda
- 1 tsp salt
- 1 cup pretzel pieces
- 1/2 cup caramel bits
- Flaked sea salt, for sprinkling

Instructions:

1. Preheat your oven to 350°F (175°C) and line a baking sheet with parchment paper.
2. In a large mixing bowl, cream together the butter and sugars until smooth.
3. Beat in the eggs, one at a time, followed by the vanilla extract.
4. In a separate bowl, whisk together the flour, baking soda, and salt.
5. Gradually add the dry mixture to the butter mixture and mix until well combined.
6. Stir in the pretzel pieces and caramel bits.
7. Drop rounded spoonfuls of dough onto the prepared baking sheet.
8. Bake for 8-10 minutes, or until the edges are lightly golden.
9. Sprinkle with flaked sea salt and allow the cookies to cool on the baking sheet for a few minutes before transferring to a wire rack to cool completely.

Lavender Shortbread Cookies

Ingredients:

- 1 cup unsalted butter, softened
- 2/3 cup confectioners' sugar
- 1 tsp lavender extract
- 2 1/2 cups all-purpose flour
- 1/2 tsp salt

Instructions:

1. Preheat your oven to 350°F (175°C) and line a baking sheet with parchment paper.
2. In a large mixing bowl, cream together the butter and confectioners' sugar until smooth.
3. Mix in the lavender extract.
4. In a separate bowl, whisk together the flour and salt.
5. Gradually add the dry mixture to the butter mixture and mix until a dough forms.
6. Roll the dough into small balls and place them on the prepared baking sheet.
7. Flatten the balls slightly with the back of a fork and bake for 12-15 minutes, or until the edges are lightly golden.
8. Allow the cookies to cool on the baking sheet for a few minutes before transferring to a wire rack to cool completely.

Matcha Green Tea Cookies

Ingredients:

- 1 cup unsalted butter, softened
- 1 cup sugar
- 2 large eggs
- 2 cups all-purpose flour
- 1 tsp baking powder
- 1 tsp salt
- 1 tsp matcha green tea powder
- 1 cup semisweet chocolate chips

Instructions:

1. Preheat your oven to 350°F (175°C) and line a baking sheet with parchment paper.
2. In a large mixing bowl, beat together the butter and sugar until well combined.
3. Beat in the eggs.
4. In a separate bowl, whisk together the flour, baking powder, salt, and matcha green tea powder.
5. Gradually add the dry mixture to the butter mixture and mix until well combined.
6. Stir in the chocolate chips.
7. Drop rounded spoonfuls of dough onto the prepared baking sheet.
8. Bake for 10-12 minutes, or until the edges are lightly golden.
9. Allow the cookies to cool on the baking sheet for a few minutes before transferring to a wire rack to cool completely.

Lavender Honey Cookies

Ingredients:

- 1 cup butter, softened
- 1 cup white sugar
- 1 egg
- 2 tablespoons honey
- 2 teaspoons dried lavender
- 3 cups all-purpose flour
- 1 teaspoon baking powder
- 1/2 teaspoon salt

Instructions:

1. Preheat your oven to 350°F (180°C).
2. In a large mixing bowl, cream together the butter and sugar until smooth. Beat in the egg and honey until well combined.
3. In a separate small bowl, mix together the lavender, flour, baking powder, and salt. Gradually add this dry mixture to the wet mixture and mix until well combined.
4. Drop spoonfuls of the dough onto ungreased baking sheets, leaving about 2 inches of space between each cookie.
5. Bake for 8-10 minutes, or until the edges of the cookies are lightly golden.
6. Allow the cookies to cool on the baking sheet for a few minutes before transferring them to a wire rack to cool completely.

Red Bean Paste Cookies

Ingredients:

- 1 cup red bean paste
- 1/2 cup butter, softened
- 1/2 cup white sugar
- 1 egg
- 1 3/4 cups all-purpose flour
- 1 teaspoon baking powder
- 1/2 teaspoon salt

Instructions:

1. Preheat your oven to 350°F (180°C).
2. In a large mixing bowl, beat together the red bean paste, butter, and sugar until smooth. Beat in the egg until well combined.
3. In a separate small bowl, mix together the flour, baking powder, and salt. Gradually add this dry mixture to the wet mixture and mix until well combined.
4. Drop spoonfuls of the dough onto ungreased baking sheets, leaving about 2 inches of space between each cookie.
5. Bake for 8-10 minutes, or until the edges of the cookies are lightly golden.
6. Allow the cookies to cool on the baking sheet for a few minutes before transferring them to a wire rack to cool completely. Enjoy!

Avocado Cookies

Ingredients:

- 1 cup mashed avocado
- 1 cup white sugar
- 1 egg
- 1 teaspoon vanilla extract
- 2 cups all-purpose flour
- 1 teaspoon baking powder
- 1/2 teaspoon salt

Instructions:

1. Preheat your oven to 350°F (180°C).
2. In a large mixing bowl, beat together the mashed avocado, sugar, egg, and vanilla extract until smooth.
3. In a separate small bowl, mix together the flour, baking powder, and salt. Gradually add this dry mixture to the wet mixture and mix until well combined.
4. Drop spoonfuls of the dough onto ungreased baking sheets, leaving about 2 inches of space between each cookie.
5. Bake for 8-10 minutes, or until the edges of the cookies are lightly golden.
6. Allow the cookies to cool on the baking sheet for a few minutes before transferring them to a wire rack to cool completely. Enjoy!

Black Licorice Cookies

Ingredients:

- 1 cup butter, softened
- 1 cup white sugar
- 1 egg
- 2 cups all-purpose flour
- 1 teaspoon baking powder
- 1/2 teaspoon salt
- 1 cup chopped black licorice candy

Instructions:

1. Preheat your oven to 350°F (180°C).
2. In a large mixing bowl, cream together the butter and sugar until smooth. Beat in the egg until well combined.
3. In a separate small bowl, mix together the flour, baking powder, and salt. Gradually add this dry mixture to the wet mixture and mix until well combined. Stir in the chopped black licorice candy.
4. Drop spoonfuls of the dough onto ungreased baking sheets, leaving about 2 inches of space between each cookie.
5. Bake for 8-10 minutes, or until the edges of the cookies are lightly golden.
6. Allow the cookies to cool on the baking sheet for a few minutes before transferring them to a wire rack to cool completely. Enjoy!

Matcha White Chocolate Cookies

Ingredients:

- 1 cup butter, softened
- 1 cup white sugar
- 1 egg
- 1 teaspoon matcha green tea powder
- 2 cups all-purpose flour
- 1 teaspoon baking powder
- 1/2 teaspoon salt
- 1 cup white chocolate chips

Instructions:

1. Preheat your oven to 350°F (180°C).
2. In a large mixing bowl, cream together the butter and sugar until smooth. Beat in the egg and matcha powder until well combined.
3. In a separate small bowl, mix together the flour, baking powder, and salt. Gradually add this dry mixture to the wet mixture and mix until well combined. Stir in the white chocolate chips.
4. Drop spoonfuls of the dough onto ungreased baking sheets, leaving about 2 inches of space between each cookie.
5. Bake for 8-10 minutes, or until the edges of the cookies are lightly golden.
6. Allow the cookies to cool on the baking sheet for a few minutes before transferring them to a wire rack to cool completely. Enjoy!

Rosewater Shortbread Cookies

Ingredients:

- 1 cup butter, softened
- 1/2 cup white sugar
- 2 tablespoons rosewater
- 2 cups all-purpose flour
- 1/4 teaspoon salt

Instructions:

1. Preheat your oven to 325°F (160°C).
2. In a large mixing bowl, cream together the butter and sugar until smooth. Beat in the rosewater until well combined.
3. In a separate small bowl, mix together the flour and salt. Gradually add this dry mixture to the wet mixture and mix until well combined.
4. Roll the dough into a log shape and slice it into 1/4-inch thick rounds. Place the rounds onto ungreased baking sheets, leaving about 1 inch of space between each cookie.
5. Bake for 15-20 minutes, or until the edges of the cookies are lightly golden.
6. Allow the cookies to cool on the baking sheet for a few minutes before transferring them to a wire rack to cool completely. Enjoy!

Cornflake Cookies

Ingredients:

- 1 cup butter, softened
- 1 cup white sugar
- 1 egg
- 1 teaspoon vanilla extract
- 1 1/2 cups all-purpose flour
- 1 cup crushed cornflakes
- 1/2 teaspoon baking powder
- 1/4 teaspoon salt

Instructions:

1. Preheat your oven to 350°F (180°C).
2. In a large mixing bowl, cream together the butter and sugar until smooth. Beat in the egg and vanilla extract until well combined.
3. In a separate small bowl, mix together the flour, crushed cornflakes, baking powder, and salt. Gradually add this dry mixture to the wet mixture and mix until well combined.
4. Drop spoonfuls of the dough onto ungreased baking sheets, leaving about 2 inches of space between each cookie.
5. Bake for 8-10 minutes, or until the edges of the cookies are lightly golden.
6. Allow the cookies to cool on the baking sheet for a few minutes before transferring them to a wire rack to cool completely. Enjoy!

Sweet Potato Cookies

Ingredients:

- 1 cup mashed sweet potatoes
- 1/2 cup butter, softened
- 1/2 cup white sugar
- 1 egg
- 1 teaspoon vanilla extract
- 1 1/2 cups all-purpose flour
- 1 teaspoon baking powder
- 1/4 teaspoon salt
- 1/2 cup chopped pecans (optional)

Instructions:

1. Preheat your oven to 350°F (180°C).
2. In a large mixing bowl, beat together the mashed sweet potatoes, butter, sugar, egg, and vanilla extract until smooth.
3. In a separate small bowl, mix together the flour, baking powder, and salt. Gradually add this dry mixture to the wet mixture and mix until well combined. Stir in the chopped pecans, if using.
4. Drop spoonfuls of the dough onto ungreased baking sheets, leaving about 2 inches of space between each cookie.
5. Bake for 8-10 minutes, or until the edges of the cookies are lightly golden.
6. Allow the cookies to cool on the baking sheet for a few minutes before transferring them to a wire rack to cool completely. Enjoy!

Oatmeal Raisin Cookies with Bacon

Ingredients:

- 1 cup butter, softened
- 1 cup white sugar
- 1 egg
- 1 teaspoon vanilla extract
- 2 cups all-purpose flour
- 1 cup rolled oats
- 1/2 teaspoon baking powder
- 1/2 teaspoon baking soda
- 1/2 teaspoon salt
- 1/2 cup raisins
- 4 slices cooked bacon, crumbled

Instructions:

1. Preheat your oven to 350°F (180°C).
2. In a large mixing bowl, cream together the butter and sugar until smooth. Beat in the egg and vanilla extract until well combined.
3. In a separate small bowl, mix together the flour, oats, baking powder, baking soda, and salt. Gradually add this dry mixture to the wet mixture and mix until well combined. Stir in the raisins and crumbled bacon.
4. Drop spoonfuls of the dough onto ungreased baking sheets, leaving about 2 inches of space between each cookie.
5. Bake for 8-10 minutes, or until the edges of the cookies are lightly golden.
6. Allow the cookies to cool on the baking sheet for a few minutes before transferring them to a wire rack to cool completely. Enjoy!

Peanut Butter and Jelly Cookies

Ingredients:

- 1 cup peanut butter
- 1 cup white sugar
- 1 egg
- 1 teaspoon vanilla extract
- 1 1/2 cups all-purpose flour
- 1/2 teaspoon baking powder
- 1/4 teaspoon salt
- 1/2 cup raspberry jam or jelly

Instructions:

1. Preheat your oven to 350°F (180°C).
2. In a large mixing bowl, beat together the peanut butter, sugar, egg, and vanilla extract until smooth.
3. In a separate small bowl, mix together the flour, baking powder, and salt. Gradually add this dry mixture to the wet mixture and mix until well combined.
4. Drop spoonfuls of the dough onto ungreased baking sheets, leaving about 2 inches of space between each cookie. Make a small indentation in the center of each cookie with your thumb or the back of a spoon.
5. Fill the indentations with about 1/4 teaspoon of jam or jelly.
6. Bake for 8-10 minutes, or until the edges of the cookies are lightly golden.
7. Allow the cookies to cool on the baking sheet for a few minutes before transferring them to a wire rack to cool completely. Enjoy!

Mango Lassi Cookies

Ingredients:

- 1 cup butter, softened
- 1 cup white sugar
- 1 egg
- 1 cup mashed mango
- 1/4 cup lassi (yogurt-based drink)
- 2 cups all-purpose flour
- 1 teaspoon baking powder
- 1/2 teaspoon salt

Instructions:

1. Preheat your oven to 350°F (180°C).
2. In a large mixing bowl, cream together the butter and sugar until smooth. Beat in the egg, mashed mango, and lassi until well combined.
3. In a separate small bowl, mix together the flour, baking powder, and salt. Gradually add this dry mixture to the wet mixture and mix until well combined.
4. Drop spoonfuls of the dough onto ungreased baking sheets, leaving about 2 inches of space between each cookie.
5. Bake for 8-10 minutes, or until the edges of the cookies are lightly golden.
6. Allow the cookies to cool on the baking sheet for a few minutes before transferring them to a wire rack to cool completely. Enjoy!

Lemon and Lavender Cookies

Ingredients:

- 1 cup butter, softened
- 1 cup white sugar
- 1 egg
- 2 tablespoons lemon juice
- 2 teaspoons dried lavender flowers
- 2 cups all-purpose flour
- 1 teaspoon baking powder
- 1/2 teaspoon salt

Instructions:

1. Preheat your oven to 350°F (180°C).
2. In a large mixing bowl, cream together the butter and sugar until smooth. Beat in the egg, lemon juice, and lavender flowers until well combined.
3. In a separate small bowl, mix together the flour, baking powder, and salt. Gradually add this dry mixture to the wet mixture and mix until well combined.
4. Drop spoonfuls of the dough onto ungreased baking sheets, leaving about 2 inches of space between each cookie.
5. Bake for 8-10 minutes, or until the edges of the cookies are lightly golden.
6. Allow the cookies to cool on the baking sheet for a few minutes before transferring them to a wire rack to cool completely. Enjoy!

Sweet Potato and Marshmallow Cookies

Ingredients:

- 1 cup butter, softened
- 1 cup white sugar
- 1 egg
- 1 cup mashed sweet potato
- 2 cups all-purpose flour
- 1 teaspoon baking powder
- 1/2 teaspoon salt
- 1 cup mini marshmallows

Instructions:

1. Preheat your oven to 350°F (180°C).
2. In a large mixing bowl, cream together the butter and sugar until smooth. Beat in the egg and mashed sweet potato until well combined.
3. In a separate small bowl, mix together the flour, baking powder, and salt. Gradually add this dry mixture to the wet mixture and mix until well combined. Stir in the mini marshmallows.
4. Drop spoonfuls of the dough onto ungreased baking sheets, leaving about 2 inches of space between each cookie.
5. Bake for 8-10 minutes, or until the edges of the cookies are lightly golden.
6. Allow the cookies to cool on the baking sheet for a few minutes before transferring them to a wire rack to cool completely. Enjoy!

Rosewater Almond Cookies

Ingredients:

- 1 cup butter, softened
- 1 cup white sugar
- 1 egg
- 1 teaspoon rosewater
- 2 cups all-purpose flour
- 1 teaspoon baking powder
- 1/2 teaspoon salt
- 1 cup finely chopped almonds

Instructions:

1. Preheat your oven to 350°F (180°C).
2. In a large mixing bowl, cream together the butter and sugar until smooth. Beat in the egg and rosewater until well combined.
3. In a separate small bowl, mix together the flour, baking powder, and salt. Gradually add this dry mixture to the wet mixture and mix until well combined. Stir in the chopped almonds.
4. Drop spoonfuls of the dough onto ungreased baking sheets, leaving about 2 inches of space between each cookie.
5. Bake for 8-10 minutes, or until the edges of the cookies are lightly golden.
6. Allow the cookies to cool on the baking sheet for a few minutes before transferring them to a wire rack to cool completely. Enjoy!

Saffron Cardamom Cookies

Ingredients:

- 1 cup butter, softened
- 1 cup white sugar
- 1 egg
- 1/2 teaspoon saffron threads, crushed
- 1/2 teaspoon ground cardamom
- 2 cups all-purpose flour
- 1/2 teaspoon baking powder
- 1/4 teaspoon salt

Instructions:

1. Preheat your oven to 350°F (180°C).
2. In a large mixing bowl, cream together the butter and sugar until smooth. Beat in the egg, crushed saffron, and ground cardamom until well combined.
3. In a separate small bowl, mix together the flour, baking powder, and salt. Gradually add this dry mixture to the wet mixture and mix until well combined.
4. Drop spoonfuls of the dough onto ungreased baking sheets, leaving about 2 inches of space between each cookie.
5. Bake for 8-10 minutes, or until the edges of the cookies are lightly golden.
6. Allow the cookies to cool on the baking sheet for a few minutes before transferring them to a wire rack to cool completely. Enjoy!

SPICING THINGS UP

Cookies With Unexpected Spices

Spicy Cheddar Cookies

Ingredients:

- 1 cup unsalted butter, softened
- 1 cup grated cheddar cheese
- 1 cup sugar
- 2 large eggs
- 2 cups all-purpose flour
- 1 tsp baking powder
- 1 tsp salt
- 1 tsp chili powder
- 1 tsp paprika

Instructions:

1. Preheat your oven to 350°F (175°C) and line a baking sheet with parchment paper.
2. In a large mixing bowl, beat together the butter, cheddar cheese, and sugar until well combined.
3. Beat in the eggs.
4. In a separate bowl, whisk together the flour, baking powder, salt, chili powder, and paprika.
5. Gradually add the dry mixture to the butter mixture and mix until well combined.
6. Drop rounded spoonfuls of dough onto the prepared baking sheet.
7. Bake for 10-12 minutes, or until the edges are lightly golden.
8. Allow the cookies to cool on the baking sheet for a few minutes before transferring to a wire rack to cool completely.

Spicy Chocolate Chipotle Cookies

Ingredients:

- 1 cup butter, softened
- 1 cup white sugar
- 1 egg
- 1 teaspoon vanilla extract
- 2 cups all-purpose flour
- 1 teaspoon baking powder
- 1/2 teaspoon salt
- 1 cup semisweet chocolate chips
- 2 tablespoons chipotle peppers in adobo sauce, finely chopped

Instructions:

1. Preheat your oven to 350°F (180°C).
2. In a large mixing bowl, cream together the butter and sugar until smooth. Beat in the egg and vanilla extract until well combined.
3. In a separate small bowl, mix together the flour, baking powder, and salt. Gradually add this dry mixture to the wet mixture and mix until well combined. Stir in the chocolate chips and finely chopped chipotle peppers.
4. Drop spoonfuls of the dough onto ungreased baking sheets, leaving about 2 inches of space between each cookie.
5. Bake for 8-10 minutes, or until the edges of the cookies are lightly golden.
6. Allow the cookies to cool on the baking sheet for a few minutes before transferring them to a wire rack to cool completely. Enjoy!

Spicy Mexican Hot Chocolate Cookies

Ingredients:

- 1 cup butter, softened
- 1 cup white sugar
- 1 egg
- 1 teaspoon vanilla extract
- 2 cups all-purpose flour
- 1 teaspoon baking powder
- 1/2 teaspoon salt
- 1 cup semisweet chocolate chips
- 2 tablespoons unsweetened cocoa powder
- 1 teaspoon ground cinnamon
- 1/2 teaspoon cayenne pepper
- 1/4 teaspoon ground cloves

Instructions:

1. Preheat your oven to 350°F (180°C).
2. In a large mixing bowl, cream together the butter and sugar until smooth. Beat in the egg and vanilla extract until well combined.
3. In a separate small bowl, mix together the flour, baking powder, and salt. Gradually add this dry mixture to the wet mixture and mix until well combined. Stir in the chocolate chips, cocoa powder, cinnamon, cayenne pepper, and cloves.
4. Drop spoonfuls of the dough onto ungreased baking sheets, leaving about 2 inches of space between each cookie.
5. Bake for 8-10 minutes, or until the edges of the cookies are lightly golden.
6. Allow the cookies to cool on the baking sheet for a few minutes before transferring them to a wire rack to cool completely. Enjoy!

Spicy Ancho Chili and Dark Chocolate Cookies

Ingredients:

- 1 cup butter, softened
- 1 cup white sugar
- 1 egg
- 1 teaspoon vanilla extract
- 2 cups all-purpose flour
- 1 teaspoon baking powder
- 1/2 teaspoon salt
- 1 cup dark chocolate chips
- 2 tablespoons ground ancho chili pepper
- 1/2 teaspoon ground cumin

Instructions:

1. Preheat your oven to 350°F (180°C).
2. In a large mixing bowl, cream together the butter and sugar until smooth. Beat in the egg and vanilla extract until well combined.
3. In a separate small bowl, mix together the flour, baking powder, and salt. Gradually add this dry mixture to the wet mixture and mix until well combined. Stir in the dark chocolate chips, ancho chili pepper, and cumin.
4. Drop spoonfuls of the dough onto ungreased baking sheets, leaving about 2 inches of space between each cookie.
5. Bake for 8-10 minutes, or until the edges of the cookies are lightly golden.
6. Allow the cookies to cool on the baking sheet for a few minutes before transferring them to a wire rack to cool completely. Enjoy!

Spicy Harissa and Cheddar Cookies

Ingredients:

- 1 cup butter, softened
- 1 cup white sugar
- 1 egg
- 1 teaspoon vanilla extract
- 2 cups all-purpose flour
- 1 teaspoon baking powder
- 1/2 teaspoon salt
- 1 cup shredded cheddar cheese
- 2 tablespoons harissa paste

Instructions:

1. Preheat your oven to 350°F (180°C).
2. In a large mixing bowl, cream together the butter and sugar until smooth. Beat in the egg and vanilla extract until well combined.
3. In a separate small bowl, mix together the flour, baking powder, and salt. Gradually add this dry mixture to the wet mixture and mix until well combined. Stir in the shredded cheddar cheese and harissa paste.
4. Drop spoonfuls of the dough onto ungreased baking sheets, leaving about 2 inches of space between each cookie.
5. Bake for 8-10 minutes, or until the edges of the cookies are lightly golden.
6. Allow the cookies to cool on the baking sheet for a few minutes before transferring them to a wire rack to cool completely. Enjoy!

Spicy Chili Chocolate Cookies

Ingredients:

- 1 cup unsalted butter, softened
- 1 cup sugar
- 2 large eggs
- 2 cups all-purpose flour
- 1 cup cocoa powder
- 1 tsp baking powder
- 1 tsp salt
- 1 tsp chili powder
- 1 cup semisweet chocolate chips

Instructions:

1. Preheat your oven to 350°F (175°C) and line a baking sheet with parchment paper.
2. In a large mixing bowl, beat together the butter and sugar until well combined.
3. Beat in the eggs.
4. In a separate bowl, whisk together the flour, cocoa powder, baking powder, salt, and chili powder.
5. Gradually add the dry mixture to the butter mixture and mix until well combined.
6. Stir in the chocolate chips.
7. Drop rounded spoonfuls of dough onto the prepared baking sheet.
8. Bake for 10-12 minutes, or until the edges are lightly golden.
9. Allow the cookies to cool on the baking sheet for a few minutes before transferring to a wire rack to cool completely.

Spicy Cumin and Coriander Cookies

Ingredients:

- 1 cup butter, softened
- 1 cup white sugar
- 1 egg
- 1 teaspoon vanilla extract
- 2 cups all-purpose flour
- 1 teaspoon baking powder
- 1/2 teaspoon salt
- 1 teaspoon ground cumin
- 1 teaspoon ground coriander
- 1/4 teaspoon cayenne pepper

Instructions:

1. Preheat your oven to 350°F (180°C).
2. In a large mixing bowl, cream together the butter and sugar until smooth. Beat in the egg and vanilla extract until well combined.
3. In a separate small bowl, mix together the flour, baking powder, and salt. Gradually add this dry mixture to the wet mixture and mix until well combined. Stir in the cumin, coriander, and cayenne pepper.
4. Drop spoonfuls of the dough onto ungreased baking sheets, leaving about 2 inches of space between each cookie.
5. Bake for 8-10 minutes, or until the edges of the cookies are lightly golden.
6. Allow the cookies to cool on the baking sheet for a few minutes before transferring them to a wire rack to cool completely. Enjoy!

Spicy Cardamom and Black Pepper Cookies

Ingredients:

- 1 cup butter, softened
- 1 cup white sugar
- 1 egg
- 1 teaspoon vanilla extract
- 2 cups all-purpose flour
- 1 teaspoon baking powder
- 1/2 teaspoon salt
- 1 teaspoon ground cardamom
- 1/2 teaspoon black pepper
- 1/4 teaspoon ground cloves

Instructions:

1. Preheat your oven to 350°F (180°C).
2. In a large mixing bowl, cream together the butter and sugar until smooth. Beat in the egg and vanilla extract until well combined.
3. In a separate small bowl, mix together the flour, baking powder, and salt. Gradually add this dry mixture to the wet mixture and mix until well combined. Stir in the cardamom, black pepper, and cloves.
4. Drop spoonfuls of the dough onto ungreased baking sheets, leaving about 2 inches of space between each cookie.
5. Bake for 8-10 minutes, or until the edges of the cookies are lightly golden.
6. Allow the cookies to cool on the baking sheet for a few minutes before transferring them to a wire rack to cool completely. Enjoy!

Miso Sesame Cookies

Ingredients:

- 1 cup unsalted butter, softened
- 1/2 cup white miso paste
- 1 cup sugar
- 2 large eggs
- 2 cups all-purpose flour
- 1 cup sesame seeds
- 1 tsp baking powder
- 1 tsp salt

Instructions:

1. Preheat your oven to 350°F (175°C) and line a baking sheet with parchment paper.
2. In a large mixing bowl, beat together the butter, miso paste, and sugar until well combined.
3. Beat in the eggs.
4. In a separate bowl, whisk together the flour, sesame seeds, baking powder, and salt.
5. Gradually add the dry mixture to the butter mixture and mix until well combined.
6. Drop rounded spoonfuls of dough onto the prepared baking sheet.
7. Bake for 10-12 minutes, or until the edges are lightly golden.
8. Allow the cookies to cool on the baking sheet for a few minutes before transferring to a wire rack to cool completely.

Spicy Szechuan Peppercorn and Cherry Cookies

Ingredients:

- 1 cup butter, softened
- 1 cup white sugar
- 1 egg
- 1 teaspoon vanilla extract
- 2 cups all-purpose flour
- 1 teaspoon baking powder
- 1/2 teaspoon salt
- 1 cup dried cherries
- 1 teaspoon Szechuan peppercorns, ground
- 1/2 teaspoon ground cumin

Instructions:

1. Preheat your oven to 350°F (180°C).
2. In a large mixing bowl, cream together the butter and sugar until smooth. Beat in the egg and vanilla extract until well combined.
3. In a separate small bowl, mix together the flour, baking powder, and salt. Gradually add this dry mixture to the wet mixture and mix until well combined. Stir in the dried cherries, ground Szechuan peppercorns, and cumin.
4. Drop spoonfuls of the dough onto ungreased baking sheets, leaving about 2 inches of space between each cookie.
5. Bake for 8-10 minutes, or until the edges of the cookies are lightly golden.
6. Allow the cookies to cool on the baking sheet for a few minutes before transferring them to a wire rack to cool completely. Enjoy!

Miso Butter Cookies

Ingredients:

- 1 cup unsalted butter, softened
- 1/2 cup white miso paste
- 1 cup sugar
- 2 large eggs
- 2 1/4 cups all-purpose flour
- 1 tsp baking soda
- 1 tsp salt

Instructions:

1. Preheat your oven to 350°F (175°C) and line a baking sheet with parchment paper.
2. In a large mixing bowl, beat together the butter, miso paste, and sugar until well combined.
3. Beat in the eggs.
4. In a separate bowl, whisk together the flour, baking soda, and salt.
5. Gradually add the dry mixture to the butter mixture and mix until well combined.
6. Drop rounded spoonfuls of dough onto the prepared baking sheet.
7. Bake for 10-12 minutes, or until the edges are lightly golden.
8. Allow the cookies to cool on the baking sheet for a few minutes before transferring to a wire rack to cool completely.

Spicy Gingerbread Cookies

Ingredients:

- 1 cup butter, softened
- 1 cup brown sugar
- 1 egg
- 1/2 cup molasses
- 3 cups all-purpose flour
- 2 teaspoons ground ginger
- 1 teaspoon ground cinnamon
- 1/2 teaspoon ground cloves
- 1/2 teaspoon cayenne pepper
- 1/2 teaspoon baking soda
- 1/4 teaspoon salt

Instructions:

1. Preheat your oven to 350°F (180°C).
2. In a large mixing bowl, cream together the butter and brown sugar until smooth. Beat in the egg and molasses until well combined.
3. In a separate small bowl, mix together the flour, ginger, cinnamon, cloves, cayenne pepper, baking soda, and salt. Gradually add this dry mixture to the wet mixture and mix until well combined.
4. Roll the dough out on a lightly floured surface to about 1/4-inch thickness. Use cookie cutters to cut out desired shapes and place them onto ungreased baking sheets, leaving about 1 inch of space between each cookie.
5. Bake for 8-10 minutes, or until the edges of the cookies are lightly golden.
6. Allow the cookies to cool on the baking sheet for a few minutes before transferring them to a wire rack to cool completely. Enjoy!

Chili Chocolate Cookies

Ingredients:

- 1 cup butter, softened
- 1 cup white sugar
- 1 egg
- 1 teaspoon chili powder
- 2 cups all-purpose flour
- 1 teaspoon baking powder
- 1/2 teaspoon salt
- 1 cup dark chocolate chips

Instructions:

1. Preheat your oven to 350°F (180°C).
2. In a large mixing bowl, cream together the butter and sugar until smooth. Beat in the egg and chili powder until well combined.
3. In a separate small bowl, mix together the flour, baking powder, and salt. Gradually add this dry mixture to the wet mixture and mix until well combined. Stir in the dark chocolate chips.
4. Drop spoonfuls of the dough onto ungreased baking sheets, leaving about 2 inches of space between each cookie.
5. Bake for 8-10 minutes, or until the edges of the cookies are lightly golden.
6. Allow the cookies to cool on the baking sheet for a few minutes before transferring them to a wire rack to cool completely. Enjoy!

Miso Caramel Cookies

Ingredients:

- 1 cup butter, softened
- 1 cup white sugar
- 1 egg
- 1 tablespoon miso paste
- 2 cups all-purpose flour
- 1 teaspoon baking powder
- 1/2 teaspoon salt
- 1/2 cup caramel candies

Instructions:

1. Preheat your oven to 350°F (180°C).
2. In a large mixing bowl, cream together the butter and sugar until smooth. Beat in the egg and miso paste until well combined.
3. In a separate small bowl, mix together the flour, baking powder, and salt. Gradually add this dry mixture to the wet mixture and mix until well combined.
4. Roll spoonfuls of the dough into balls and press a caramel candy into the center of each ball. Press the dough around the candy to enclose it completely.
5. Place the balls of dough onto ungreased baking sheets, leaving about 2 inches of space between each cookie.
6. Bake for 8-10 minutes, or until the edges of the cookies are lightly golden.
7. Allow the cookies to cool on the baking sheet for a few minutes before transferring them to a wire rack to cool completely. Enjoy!

Curry Cookies

Ingredients:

- 1 cup butter, softened
- 1 cup white sugar
- 1 egg
- 1 teaspoon curry powder
- 2 cups all-purpose flour
- 1 teaspoon baking powder
- 1/2 teaspoon salt

Instructions:

1. Preheat your oven to 350°F (180°C).
2. In a large mixing bowl, cream together the butter and sugar until smooth. Beat in the egg until well combined.
3. In a separate small bowl, mix together the curry powder, flour, baking powder, and salt. Gradually add this dry mixture to the wet mixture and mix until well combined.
4. Drop spoonfuls of the dough onto ungreased baking sheets, leaving about 2 inches of space between each cookie.
5. Bake for 8-10 minutes, or until the edges of the cookies are lightly golden.
6. Allow the cookies to cool on the baking sheet for a few minutes before transferring them to a wire rack to cool completely.

Wasabi Pea Cookies

Ingredients:

- 1 cup butter, softened
- 1 cup white sugar
- 1 egg
- 2 cups all-purpose flour
- 1 teaspoon baking powder
- 1/2 teaspoon salt
- 1 cup crushed wasabi peas

Instructions:

1. Preheat your oven to 350°F (180°C).
2. In a large mixing bowl, cream together the butter and sugar until smooth. Beat in the egg until well combined.
3. In a separate small bowl, mix together the flour, baking powder, and salt. Gradually add this dry mixture to the wet mixture and mix until well combined. Stir in the crushed wasabi peas.
4. Drop spoonfuls of the dough onto ungreased baking sheets, leaving about 2 inches of space between each cookie.
5. Bake for 8-10 minutes, or until the edges of the cookies are lightly golden.
6. Allow the cookies to cool on the baking sheet for a few minutes before transferring them to a wire rack to cool completely. Enjoy!

Wasabi Pea and Pickle Cookies

Ingredients:

- 1 cup butter, softened
- 1 cup white sugar
- 1 egg
- 2 cups all-purpose flour
- 1 teaspoon baking powder
- 1/2 teaspoon salt
- 1 cup crushed wasabi peas
- 1/2 cup diced dill pickles

Instructions:

1. Preheat your oven to 350°F (180°C).
2. In a large mixing bowl, cream together the butter and sugar until smooth. Beat in the egg until well combined.
3. In a separate small bowl, mix together the flour, baking powder, and salt. Gradually add this dry mixture to the wet mixture and mix until well combined. Stir in the crushed wasabi peas and diced dill pickles.
4. Drop spoonfuls of the dough onto ungreased baking sheets, leaving about 2 inches of space between each cookie.
5. Bake for 8-10 minutes, or until the edges of the cookies are lightly golden.
6. Allow the cookies to cool on the baking sheet for a few minutes before transferring them to a wire rack to cool completely. Enjoy!

Wasabi Ginger Cookies

Ingredients:

- 1 cup butter, softened
- 1 cup white sugar
- 1 egg
- 2 tablespoons wasabi powder
- 2 teaspoons ground ginger
- 3 cups all-purpose flour
- 1 teaspoon baking soda
- 1/2 teaspoon salt

Instructions:

1. Preheat your oven to 350°F (180°C).
2. In a large mixing bowl, cream together the butter and sugar until smooth. Beat in the egg until well combined.
3. In a separate small bowl, mix together the wasabi powder, ginger, flour, baking soda, and salt. Gradually add this dry mixture to the wet mixture and mix until well combined.
4. Drop spoonfuls of the dough onto ungreased baking sheets, leaving about 2 inches of space between each cookie.
5. Bake for 8-10 minutes, or until the edges of the cookies are lightly golden.
6. Allow the cookies to cool on the baking sheet for a few minutes before transferring them to a wire rack to cool completely.

Curry Coconut Cookies

Ingredients:

- 1 cup unsalted butter, softened
- 1 cup sugar
- 2 large eggs
- 2 cups all-purpose flour
- 1 tsp baking powder
- 1 tsp salt
- 1 tsp curry powder
- 1 cup unsweetened coconut flakes

Instructions:

1. Preheat your oven to 350°F (175°C) and line a baking sheet with parchment paper.
2. In a large mixing bowl, beat together the butter and sugar until well combined.
3. Beat in the eggs.
4. In a separate bowl, whisk together the flour, baking powder, salt, and curry powder.
5. Gradually add the dry mixture to the butter mixture and mix until well combined.
6. Stir in the coconut flakes.
7. Drop rounded spoonfuls of dough onto the prepared baking sheet.
8. Bake for 10-12 minutes, or until the edges are lightly golden.
9. Allow the cookies to cool on the baking sheet for a few minutes before transferring to a wire rack to cool completely.

Chili Chocolate and Bacon Cookies

Ingredients:

- 1 cup butter, softened
- 1 cup white sugar
- 1 egg
- 1 teaspoon chili powder
- 2 cups all-purpose flour
- 1 teaspoon baking powder
- 1/2 teaspoon salt
- 1 cup dark chocolate chips
- 4 slices cooked bacon, crumbled

Instructions:

1. Preheat your oven to 350°F (180°C).
2. In a large mixing bowl, cream together the butter and sugar until smooth. Beat in the egg and chili powder until well combined.
3. In a separate small bowl, mix together the flour, baking powder, and salt. Gradually add this dry mixture to the wet mixture and mix until well combined. Stir in the dark chocolate chips and crumbled bacon.
4. Drop spoonfuls of the dough onto ungreased baking sheets, leaving about 2 inches of space between each cookie.
5. Bake for 8-10 minutes, or until the edges of the cookies are lightly golden.
6. Allow the cookies to cool on the baking sheet for a few minutes before transferring them to a wire rack to cool completely. Enjoy!

CAFFEINE COMMITMENT

Cookies Inspired by Coffee Flavors

Mocha Cookies

Ingredients:

- 1 cup butter, softened
- 1 cup white sugar
- 1 egg
- 2 tablespoons strong coffee
- 2 tablespoons unsweetened cocoa powder
- 2 cups all-purpose flour
- 1 teaspoon baking powder
- 1/2 teaspoon salt
- 1 cup chocolate chips

Instructions:

1. Preheat your oven to 350°F (180°C).
2. In a large mixing bowl, cream together the butter and sugar until smooth. Beat in the egg, coffee, and cocoa powder until well combined.
3. In a separate small bowl, mix together the flour, baking powder, and salt. Gradually add this dry mixture to the wet mixture and mix until well combined. Stir in the chocolate chips.
4. Drop spoonfuls of the dough onto ungreased baking sheets, leaving about 2 inches of space between each cookie.
5. Bake for 8-10 minutes, or until the edges of the cookies are lightly golden.
6. Allow the cookies to cool on the baking sheet for a few minutes before transferring them to a wire rack to cool completely. Enjoy!

Espresso and Dark Chocolate Cookies

Ingredients:

- 1 cup butter, softened
- 1 cup white sugar
- 1 egg
- 2 tablespoons espresso
- 2 cups all-purpose flour
- 1 teaspoon baking powder
- 1/2 teaspoon salt
- 1 cup dark chocolate chips

Instructions:

1. Preheat your oven to 350°F (180°C).
2. In a large mixing bowl, cream together the butter and sugar until smooth. Beat in the egg and espresso until well combined.
3. In a separate small bowl, mix together the flour, baking powder, and salt. Gradually add this dry mixture to the wet mixture and mix until well combined. Stir in the dark chocolate chips.
4. Drop spoonfuls of the dough onto ungreased baking sheets, leaving about 2 inches of space between each cookie.
5. Bake for 8-10 minutes, or until the edges of the cookies are lightly golden.
6. Allow the cookies to cool on the baking sheet for a few minutes before transferring them to a wire rack to cool completely. Enjoy!

Coffee and Cardamom Cookies

Ingredients:

- 1 cup butter, softened
- 1 cup white sugar
- 1 egg
- 2 tablespoons strong coffee
- 1 teaspoon ground cardamom
- 2 cups all-purpose flour
- 1 teaspoon baking powder
- 1/2 teaspoon salt

Instructions:

1. Preheat your oven to 350°F (180°C).
2. In a large mixing bowl, cream together the butter and sugar until smooth. Beat in the egg, coffee, and cardamom until well combined.
3. In a separate small bowl, mix together the flour, baking powder, and salt. Gradually add this dry mixture to the wet mixture and mix until well combined.
4. Drop spoonfuls of the dough onto ungreased baking sheets, leaving about 2 inches of space between each cookie.
5. Bake for 8-10 minutes, or until the edges of the cookies are lightly golden.
6. Allow the cookies to cool on the baking sheet for a few minutes before transferring them to a wire rack to cool completely. Enjoy!

Cold Brew and Coconut Cookies

Ingredients:

- 1 cup butter, softened
- 1 cup white sugar
- 1 egg
- 2 tablespoons cold brew coffee
- 2 cups all-purpose flour
- 1 teaspoon baking powder
- 1/2 teaspoon salt
- 1 cup shredded coconut

Instructions:

1. Preheat your oven to 350°F (180°C).
2. In a large mixing bowl, cream together the butter and sugar until smooth. Beat in the egg and cold brew coffee until well combined.
3. In a separate small bowl, mix together the flour, baking powder, and salt. Gradually add this dry mixture to the wet mixture and mix until well combined. Stir in the shredded coconut.
4. Drop spoonfuls of the dough onto ungreased baking sheets, leaving about 2 inches of space between each cookie.
5. Bake for 8-10 minutes, or until the edges of the cookies are lightly golden.
6. Allow the cookies to cool on the baking sheet for a few minutes before transferring them to a wire rack to cool completely. Enjoy!

Caramel Macchiato Cookies

Ingredients:

- 1 cup butter, softened
- 1 cup white sugar
- 1 egg
- 2 tablespoons caramel syrup
- 2 tablespoons strong coffee
- 2 cups all-purpose flour
- 1 teaspoon baking powder
- 1/2 teaspoon salt
- 1 cup white chocolate chips

Instructions:

1. Preheat your oven to 350°F (180°C).
2. In a large mixing bowl, cream together the butter and sugar until smooth. Beat in the egg, caramel syrup, and coffee until well combined.
3. In a separate small bowl, mix together the flour, baking powder, and salt. Gradually add this dry mixture to the wet mixture and mix until well combined. Stir in the white chocolate chips.
4. Drop spoonfuls of the dough onto ungreased baking sheets, leaving about 2 inches of space between each cookie.
5. Bake for 8-10 minutes, or until the edges of the cookies are lightly golden.
6. Allow the cookies to cool on the baking sheet for a few minutes before transferring them to a wire rack to cool completely. Enjoy!

French Press and Maple Cookies

Ingredients:

- 1 cup butter, softened
- 1 cup white sugar
- 1 egg
- 2 tablespoons maple syrup
- 2 tablespoons strong coffee brewed with a French press
- 2 cups all-purpose flour
- 1 teaspoon baking powder
- 1/2 teaspoon salt
- 1 cup chopped pecans

Instructions:

1. Preheat your oven to 350°F (180°C).
2. In a large mixing bowl, cream together the butter and sugar until smooth. Beat in the egg, maple syrup, and coffee until well combined.
3. In a separate small bowl, mix together the flour, baking powder, and salt. Gradually add this dry mixture to the wet mixture and mix until well combined. Stir in the chopped pecans.
4. Drop spoonfuls of the dough onto ungreased baking sheets, leaving about 2 inches of space between each cookie.
5. Bake for 8-10 minutes, or until the edges of the cookies are lightly golden.
6. Allow the cookies to cool on the baking sheet for a few minutes before transferring them to a wire rack to cool completely. Enjoy!

Coffee and Caramel Cookies

Ingredients:

- 1 cup butter, softened
- 1 cup white sugar
- 1 egg
- 2 tablespoons strong coffee
- 2 cups all-purpose flour
- 1 teaspoon baking powder
- 1/2 teaspoon salt
- 1 cup caramel bits

Instructions:

1. Preheat your oven to 350°F (180°C).
2. In a large mixing bowl, cream together the butter and sugar until smooth. Beat in the egg and coffee until well combined.
3. In a separate small bowl, mix together the flour, baking powder, and salt. Gradually add this dry mixture to the wet mixture and mix until well combined. Stir in the caramel bits.
4. Drop spoonfuls of the dough onto ungreased baking sheets, leaving about 2 inches of space between each cookie.
5. Bake for 8-10 minutes, or until the edges of the cookies are lightly golden.
6. Allow the cookies to cool on the baking sheet for a few minutes before transferring them to a wire rack to cool completely. Enjoy!

Vietnamese Iced Coffee Cookies

Ingredients:

- 1 cup butter, softened
- 1 cup white sugar
- 1 egg
- 2 tablespoons strong coffee
- 2 tablespoons sweetened condensed milk
- 2 cups all-purpose flour
- 1 teaspoon baking powder
- 1/2 teaspoon salt

Instructions:

1. Preheat your oven to 350°F (180°C).
2. In a large mixing bowl, cream together the butter and sugar until smooth. Beat in the egg, coffee, and sweetened condensed milk until well combined.
3. In a separate small bowl, mix together the flour, baking powder, and salt. Gradually add this dry mixture to the wet mixture and mix until well combined.
4. Drop spoonfuls of the dough onto ungreased baking sheets, leaving about 2 inches of space between each cookie.
5. Bake for 8-10 minutes, or until the edges of the cookies are lightly golden.
6. Allow the cookies to cool on the baking sheet for a few minutes before transferring them to a wire rack to cool completely. Enjoy!

Coffee and Toffee Cookies

Ingredients:

- 1 cup butter, softened
- 1 cup white sugar
- 1 egg
- 2 tablespoons strong coffee
- 2 cups all-purpose flour
- 1 teaspoon baking powder
- 1/2 teaspoon salt
- 1 cup toffee bits

Instructions:

1. Preheat your oven to 350°F (180°C).
2. In a large mixing bowl, cream together the butter and sugar until smooth. Beat in the egg and coffee until well combined.
3. In a separate small bowl, mix together the flour, baking powder, and salt. Gradually add this dry mixture to the wet mixture and mix until well combined. Stir in the toffee bits.
4. Drop spoonfuls of the dough onto ungreased baking sheets, leaving about 2 inches of space between each cookie.
5. Bake for 8-10 minutes, or until the edges of the cookies are lightly golden.
6. Allow the cookies to cool on the baking sheet for a few minutes before transferring them to a wire rack to cool completely. Enjoy!

Coffee and Gingerbread Cookies

Ingredients:

- 1 cup butter, softened
- 1 cup white sugar
- 1 egg
- 2 tablespoons strong coffee
- 1 teaspoon ground ginger
- 1 teaspoon ground cinnamon
- 1/2 teaspoon ground cloves
- 2 cups all-purpose flour
- 1 teaspoon baking powder
- 1/2 teaspoon salt

Instructions:

1. Preheat your oven to 350°F (180°C).
2. In a large mixing bowl, cream together the butter and sugar until smooth. Beat in the egg, coffee, ginger, cinnamon, and cloves until well combined.
3. In a separate small bowl, mix together the flour, baking powder, and salt. Gradually add this dry mixture to the wet mixture and mix until well combined.
4. Drop spoonfuls of the dough onto ungreased baking sheets, leaving about 2 inches of space between each cookie.
5. Bake for 8-10 minutes, or until the edges of the cookies are lightly golden.
6. Allow the cookies to cool on the baking sheet for a few minutes before transferring them to a wire rack to cool completely. Enjoy!

Coffee and Nutella Cookies

Ingredients:

- 1 cup butter, softened
- 1 cup white sugar
- 1 egg
- 2 tablespoons strong coffee
- 2 cups all-purpose flour
- 1 teaspoon baking powder
- 1/2 teaspoon salt
- 1 cup Nutella

Instructions:

1. Preheat your oven to 350°F (180°C).
2. In a large mixing bowl, cream together the butter and sugar until smooth. Beat in the egg and coffee until well combined.
3. In a separate small bowl, mix together the flour, baking powder, and salt. Gradually add this dry mixture to the wet mixture and mix until well combined. Stir in the Nutella.
4. Drop spoonfuls of the dough onto ungreased baking sheets, leaving about 2 inches of space between each cookie.
5. Bake for 8-10 minutes, or until the edges of the cookies are lightly golden.
6. Allow the cookies to cool on the baking sheet for a few minutes before transferring them to a wire rack to cool completely. Enjoy!

Coffee and Vanilla Bean Cookies

Ingredients:

- 1 cup butter, softened
- 1 cup white sugar
- 1 egg
- 2 tablespoons strong coffee
- 1 vanilla bean, seeds scraped
- 2 cups all-purpose flour
- 1 teaspoon baking powder
- 1/2 teaspoon salt

Instructions:

1. Preheat your oven to 350°F (180°C).
2. In a large mixing bowl, cream together the butter and sugar until smooth. Beat in the egg, coffee, and vanilla bean seeds until well combined.
3. In a separate small bowl, mix together the flour, baking powder, and salt. Gradually add this dry mixture to the wet mixture and mix until well combined.
4. Drop spoonfuls of the dough onto ungreased baking sheets, leaving about 2 inches of space between each cookie.
5. Bake for 8-10 minutes, or until the edges of the cookies are lightly golden.
6. Allow the cookies to cool on the baking sheet for a few minutes before transferring them to a wire rack to cool completely. Enjoy!

TREATS FROM THE GROWN-UPS TABLE

Cookies With Adult Beverage Flavor Profiles

NOTE: If you are not of legal age to consume alcohol, check with an adult before trying these.

Whiskey Pecan Cookies

Ingredients:

- 1 cup unsalted butter, softened
- 1 cup sugar
- 2 large eggs
- 1/2 cup whiskey
- 2 cups all-purpose flour
- 1 tsp baking powder
- 1 tsp salt
- 1 cup chopped pecans

Instructions:

1. Preheat your oven to 350°F (175°C) and line a baking sheet with parchment paper.
2. In a large mixing bowl, beat together the butter and sugar until well combined.
3. Beat in the eggs, followed by the whiskey.
4. In a separate bowl, whisk together the flour, baking powder, and salt.
5. Gradually add the dry mixture to the butter mixture and mix until well combined.
6. Stir in the chopped pecans.
7. Drop rounded spoonfuls of dough onto the prepared baking sheet.
8. Bake for 10-12 minutes, or until the edges are lightly golden.
9. Allow the cookies to cool on the baking sheet for a few minutes before transferring to a wire rack to cool completely.

Beer Cookies

Ingredients:

- 1 cup butter, softened
- 1 cup white sugar
- 1 egg
- 1 cup beer
- 3 cups all-purpose flour
- 1 teaspoon baking powder
- 1/2 teaspoon salt

Instructions:

1. Preheat your oven to 350°F (180°C).
2. In a large mixing bowl, cream together the butter and sugar until smooth. Beat in the egg and beer until well combined.
3. In a separate small bowl, mix together the flour, baking powder, and salt. Gradually add this dry mixture to the wet mixture and mix until well combined.
4. Drop spoonfuls of the dough onto ungreased baking sheets, leaving about 2 inches of space between each cookie.
5. Bake for 8-10 minutes, or until the edges of the cookies are lightly golden.
6. Allow the cookies to cool on the baking sheet for a few minutes before transferring them to a wire rack to cool completely. Enjoy!

Bourbon and Maple Cookies

Ingredients:

- 1 cup unsalted butter, softened
- 1 cup packed brown sugar
- 2 large eggs
- 1/2 cup bourbon
- 1/2 cup maple syrup
- 2 cups all-purpose flour
- 1 tsp baking powder
- 1 tsp salt
- 1 cup chopped pecans

Instructions:

1. Preheat your oven to 350°F (175°C) and line a baking sheet with parchment paper.
2. In a large mixing bowl, beat together the butter and brown sugar until well combined.
3. Beat in the eggs, followed by the bourbon and maple syrup.
4. In a separate bowl, whisk together the flour, baking powder, and salt.
5. Gradually add the dry mixture to the butter mixture and mix until well combined.
6. Stir in the chopped pecans.
7. Drop rounded spoonfuls of dough onto the prepared baking sheet.
8. Bake for 10-12 minutes, or until the edges are lightly golden.
9. Allow the cookies to cool on the baking sheet for a few minutes before transferring to a wire rack to cool completely.

Red Wine Chocolate Cookies

Ingredients:

- 1 cup unsalted butter, softened
- 1 cup sugar
- 2 large eggs
- 1/2 cup red wine
- 2 cups all-purpose flour
- 1 cup cocoa powder
- 1 tsp baking powder
- 1 tsp salt
- 1 cup semisweet chocolate chips

Instructions:

1. Preheat your oven to 350°F (175°C) and line a baking sheet with parchment paper.
2. In a large mixing bowl, beat together the butter and sugar until well combined.
3. Beat in the eggs, one at a time, followed by the red wine.
4. In a separate bowl, whisk together the flour, cocoa powder, baking powder, and salt.
5. Gradually add the dry mixture to the butter mixture and mix until well combined.
6. Stir in the chocolate chips.
7. Drop rounded spoonfuls of dough onto the prepared baking sheet.
8. Bake for 10-12 minutes, or until the edges are lightly golden.
9. Allow the cookies to cool on the baking sheet for a few minutes before transferring to a wire rack to cool completely.

Beer and Pretzel Cookies

Ingredients:

- 1 cup unsalted butter, softened
- 1 cup sugar
- 2 large eggs
- 1 cup beer
- 2 cups all-purpose flour
- 1 cup crushed pretzel pieces
- 1 tsp baking powder
- 1 tsp salt

Instructions:

1. Preheat your oven to 350°F (175°C) and line a baking sheet with parchment paper.
2. In a large mixing bowl, beat together the butter and sugar until well combined.
3. Beat in the eggs, followed by the beer.
4. In a separate bowl, whisk together the flour, crushed pretzel pieces, baking powder, and salt.
5. Gradually add the dry mixture to the butter mixture and mix until well combined.
6. Drop rounded spoonfuls of dough onto the prepared baking sheet.
7. Bake for 10-12 minutes, or until the edges are lightly golden.
8. Allow the cookies to cool on the baking sheet for a few minutes before transferring to a wire rack to cool completely.

Tequila Sunrise Cookies

Ingredients:

- 1 cup unsalted butter, softened
- 1 cup sugar
- 2 large eggs
- 2 tbsp tequila
- 2 tbsp grenadine syrup
- 2 cups all-purpose flour
- 1 tsp baking powder
- 1 tsp salt
- 1 cup orange zest
- 1 cup semisweet chocolate chips

Instructions:

1. Preheat your oven to 350°F (175°C) and line a baking sheet with parchment paper.
2. In a large mixing bowl, beat together the butter and sugar until well combined.
3. Beat in the eggs, followed by the tequila and grenadine syrup.
4. In a separate bowl, whisk together the flour, baking powder, and salt.
5. Gradually add the dry mixture to the butter mixture and mix until well combined.
6. Stir in the orange zest and chocolate chips.
7. Drop rounded spoonfuls of dough onto the prepared baking sheet.
8. Bake for 10-12 minutes, or until the edges are lightly golden.
9. Allow the cookies to cool on the baking sheet for a few minutes before transferring to a wire rack to cool completely.

Margarita Cookies

Ingredients:

- 1 cup butter, softened
- 1 cup white sugar
- 1 egg
- 2 tablespoons tequila
- 2 tablespoons lime juice
- 2 tablespoons orange liqueur
- 2 cups all-purpose flour
- 1 teaspoon baking powder
- 1/2 teaspoon salt
- 1 cup coarse sugar (for rolling)

Instructions:

1. Preheat your oven to 350°F (180°C).
2. In a large mixing bowl, cream together the butter and sugar until smooth. Beat in the egg, tequila, lime juice, and orange liqueur until well combined.
3. In a separate small bowl, mix together the flour, baking powder, and salt. Gradually add this dry mixture to the wet mixture and mix until well combined.
4. Roll the dough into 1-inch balls and roll them in the coarse sugar. Place the balls onto ungreased baking sheets, leaving about 2 inches of space between each cookie.
5. Bake for 8-10 minutes, or until the edges of the cookies are lightly golden.
6. Allow the cookies to cool on the baking sheet for a few minutes before transferring them to a wire rack to cool completely. Enjoy!

Irish Whiskey and Baileys Cookies

Ingredients:

- 1 cup butter, softened
- 1 cup white sugar
- 1 egg
- 2 tablespoons Irish whiskey
- 2 tablespoons Baileys Irish Cream
- 2 cups all-purpose flour
- 1 teaspoon baking powder
- 1/2 teaspoon salt

Instructions:

1. Preheat your oven to 350°F (180°C).
2. In a large mixing bowl, cream together the butter and sugar until smooth. Beat in the egg, Irish whiskey, and Baileys Irish Cream until well combined.
3. In a separate small bowl, mix together the flour, baking powder, and salt. Gradually add this dry mixture to the wet mixture and mix until well combined.
4. Drop spoonfuls of the dough onto ungreased baking sheets, leaving about 2 inches of space between each cookie.
5. Bake for 8-10 minutes, or until the edges of the cookies are lightly golden.
6. Allow the cookies to cool on the baking sheet for a few minutes before transferring them to a wire rack to cool completely. Enjoy!

White Russian Cookies

Ingredients:

- 1 cup butter, softened
- 1 cup white sugar
- 1 egg
- 2 tablespoons vodka
- 2 tablespoons Kahlua
- 2 tablespoons heavy cream
- 2 cups all-purpose flour
- 1 teaspoon baking powder
- 1/2 teaspoon salt

Instructions:

1. Preheat your oven to 350°F (180°C).
2. In a large mixing bowl, cream together the butter and sugar until smooth. Beat in the egg, vodka, Kahlua, and heavy cream until well combined.
3. In a separate small bowl, mix together the flour, baking powder, and salt. Gradually add this dry mixture to the wet mixture and mix until well combined.
4. Drop spoonfuls of the dough onto ungreased baking sheets, leaving about 2 inches of space between each cookie.
5. Bake for 8-10 minutes, or until the edges of the cookies are lightly golden.
6. Allow the cookies to cool on the baking sheet for a few minutes before transferring them to a wire rack to cool completely. Enjoy!

Rum and Raisin Cookies

Ingredients:

- 1 cup butter, softened
- 1 cup white sugar
- 1 egg
- 2 tablespoons rum
- 1 cup raisins
- 2 cups all-purpose flour
- 1 teaspoon baking powder
- 1/2 teaspoon salt

Instructions:

1. Preheat your oven to 350°F (180°C).
2. In a large mixing bowl, cream together the butter and sugar until smooth. Beat in the egg and rum until well combined.
3. In a separate small bowl, mix together the flour, baking powder, and salt. Gradually add this dry mixture to the wet mixture and mix until well combined. Stir in the raisins.
4. Drop spoonfuls of the dough onto ungreased baking sheets, leaving about 2 inches of space between each cookie.
5. Bake for 8-10 minutes, or until the edges of the cookies are lightly golden.
6. Allow the cookies to cool on the baking sheet for a few minutes before transferring them to a wire rack to cool completely. Enjoy!

Kahlua and Mocha Cookies

Ingredients:

- 1 cup butter, softened
- 1 cup white sugar
- 1 egg
- 2 tablespoons Kahlua
- 2 tablespoons strong coffee
- 2 cups all-purpose flour
- 1 teaspoon baking powder
- 1/2 teaspoon salt
- 1 cup chocolate chips

Instructions:

1. Preheat your oven to 350°F (180°C).
2. In a large mixing bowl, cream together the butter and sugar until smooth. Beat in the egg, Kahlua, and coffee until well combined.
3. In a separate small bowl, mix together the flour, baking powder, and salt. Gradually add this dry mixture to the wet mixture and mix until well combined. Stir in the chocolate chips.
4. Drop spoonfuls of the dough onto ungreased baking sheets, leaving about 2 inches of space between each cookie.
5. Bake for 8-10 minutes, or until the edges of the cookies are lightly golden.
6. Allow the cookies to cool on the baking sheet for a few minutes before transferring them to a wire rack to cool completely. Enjoy!

Prosecco and Strawberry Cookies

Ingredients:

- 1 cup butter, softened
- 1 cup white sugar
- 1 egg
- 2 tablespoons Prosecco
- 1 cup diced fresh strawberries
- 2 cups all-purpose flour
- 1 teaspoon baking powder
- 1/2 teaspoon salt

Instructions:

1. Preheat your oven to 350°F (180°C).
2. In a large mixing bowl, cream together the butter and sugar until smooth. Beat in the egg and Prosecco until well combined.
3. In a separate small bowl, mix together the flour, baking powder, and salt. Gradually add this dry mixture to the wet mixture and mix until well combined. Stir in the diced strawberries.
4. Drop spoonfuls of the dough onto ungreased baking sheets, leaving about 2 inches of space between each cookie.
5. Bake for 8-10 minutes, or until the edges of the cookies are lightly golden.
6. Allow the cookies to cool on the baking sheet for a few minutes before transferring them to a wire rack to cool completely. Enjoy!

Gin and Tonic Cookies

Ingredients:

- 1 cup butter, softened
- 1 cup white sugar
- 1 egg
- 2 tablespoons gin
- 2 tablespoons tonic water
- 2 cups all-purpose flour
- 1 teaspoon baking powder
- 1/2 teaspoon salt
- 1 cup dried lime zest

Instructions:

1. Preheat your oven to 350°F (180°C).
2. In a large mixing bowl, cream together the butter and sugar until smooth. Beat in the egg, gin, and tonic water until well combined.
3. In a separate small bowl, mix together the flour, baking powder, and salt. Gradually add this dry mixture to the wet mixture and mix until well combined. Stir in the dried lime zest.
4. Drop spoonfuls of the dough onto ungreased baking sheets, leaving about 2 inches of space between each cookie.
5. Bake for 8-10 minutes, or until the edges of the cookies are lightly golden.
6. Allow the cookies to cool on the baking sheet for a few minutes before transferring them to a wire rack to cool completely. Enjoy!

Cointreau and Orange Cookies

Ingredients:

- 1 cup butter, softened
- 1 cup white sugar
- 1 egg
- 2 tablespoons Cointreau
- 2 tablespoons orange juice
- 2 cups all-purpose flour
- 1 teaspoon baking powder
- 1/2 teaspoon salt
- 1 cup chopped dried orange zest

Instructions:

1. Preheat your oven to 350°F (180°C).
2. In a large mixing bowl, cream together the butter and sugar until smooth. Beat in the egg, Cointreau, and orange juice until well combined.
3. In a separate small bowl, mix together the flour, baking powder, and salt. Gradually add this dry mixture to the wet mixture and mix until well combined. Stir in the chopped dried orange zest.
4. Drop spoonfuls of the dough onto ungreased baking sheets, leaving about 2 inches of space between each cookie.
5. Bake for 8-10 minutes, or until the edges of the cookies are lightly golden.
6. Allow the cookies to cool on the baking sheet for a few minutes before transferring them to a wire rack to cool completely. Enjoy!

Amaretto and Almond Cookies

Ingredients:

- 1 cup butter, softened
- 1 cup white sugar
- 1 egg
- 2 tablespoons Amaretto
- 2 cups all-purpose flour
- 1 teaspoon baking powder
- 1/2 teaspoon salt
- 1 cup finely chopped almonds

Instructions:

1. Preheat your oven to 350°F (180°C).
2. In a large mixing bowl, cream together the butter and sugar until smooth. Beat in the egg and Amaretto until well combined.
3. In a separate small bowl, mix together the flour, baking powder, and salt. Gradually add this dry mixture to the wet mixture and mix until well combined. Stir in the chopped almonds.
4. Drop spoonfuls of the dough onto ungreased baking sheets, leaving about 2 inches of space between each cookie.
5. Bake for 8-10 minutes, or until the edges of the cookies are lightly golden.
6. Allow the cookies to cool on the baking sheet for a few minutes before transferring them to a wire rack to cool completely. Enjoy!

CREATIVE ICING IDEAS

Add Another Layer of Customization to Your Cookies

Coffee Icing

Ingredients:

- 1 cup confectioners' sugar
- 2 tablespoons melted butter
- 2 tablespoons brewed coffee

Instructions:

1. In a medium bowl, whisk together the confectioners' sugar, melted butter, and brewed coffee.
2. Mix until the icing is smooth and spreadable.
3. Spread the icing over cooled cookies.
4. Allow the icing to set for at least 15 minutes before serving or storing the cookies.

Maple Bacon Icing

Ingredients:

- 1 cup confectioners' sugar
- 2 tablespoons maple syrup
- 2 tablespoons cooked, crumbled bacon

Instructions:

1. In a medium bowl, whisk together the confectioners' sugar, maple syrup, and crumbled bacon.
2. Mix until the icing is smooth and spreadable.
3. Spread the icing over cooled cookies.
4. Allow the icing to set for at least 15 minutes before serving or storing the cookies.

Wasabi Icing

Ingredients:

- 1 cup confectioners' sugar
- 2 tablespoons melted butter
- 1 teaspoon wasabi paste

Instructions:

1. In a medium bowl, whisk together the confectioners' sugar, melted butter, and wasabi paste.
2. Mix until the icing is smooth and spreadable.
3. Spread the icing over cooled cookies.
4. Allow the icing to set for at least 15 minutes before serving or storing the cookies.

Red Pepper Flake Icing

Ingredients:

- 1 cup confectioners' sugar
- 2 tablespoons melted butter
- 1 teaspoon red pepper flakes

Instructions:

1. In a medium bowl, whisk together the confectioners' sugar, melted butter, and red pepper flakes.
2. Mix until the icing is smooth and spreadable.
3. Spread the icing over cooled cookies.
4. Allow the icing to set for at least 15 minutes before serving or storing the cookies.

Garlic Icing

Ingredients:

- 1 cup confectioners' sugar
- 2 tablespoons melted butter
- 1 clove minced garlic

Instructions:

1. In a medium bowl, whisk together the confectioners' sugar, melted butter, and minced garlic.
2. Mix until the icing is smooth and spreadable.
3. Spread the icing over cooled cookies.
4. Allow the icing to set for at least 15 minutes before serving or storing the cookies.

Peanut Butter and Jelly Icing

Ingredients:

- 1 cup confectioners' sugar
- 2 tablespoons peanut butter
- 2 tablespoons seedless raspberry or strawberry jam

Instructions:

1. In a medium bowl, whisk together the confectioners' sugar, peanut butter, and seedless raspberry or strawberry jam.
2. Mix until the icing is smooth and spreadable.
3. Spread the icing over cooled cookies.
4. Allow the icing to set for at least 15 minutes before serving or storing the cookies.

Honey Mustard Icing

Ingredients:

- 1 cup confectioners' sugar
- 2 tablespoons honey
- 1 tablespoon mustard

Instructions:

1. In a medium bowl, whisk together the confectioners' sugar, honey, and mustard.
2. Mix until the icing is smooth and spreadable.
3. Spread the icing over cooled cookies.
4. Allow the icing to set for at least 15 minutes before serving or storing the cookies.

Gingerbread Latte Icing

Ingredients:

- 1 cup confectioners' sugar
- 2 tablespoons melted butter
- 1 tablespoon brewed coffee
- 1/4 teaspoon ginger
- 1/4 teaspoon cinnamon

Instructions:

1. In a medium bowl, whisk together the confectioners' sugar, melted butter, brewed coffee, ginger, and cinnamon.
2. Mix until the icing is smooth and spreadable.
3. Spread the icing over cooled cookies.
4. Allow the icing to set for at least 15 minutes before serving or storing the cookies.

Lavender Honey Icing

Ingredients:

- 1 cup confectioners' sugar
- 2 tablespoons honey
- 1/4 teaspoon lavender extract

Instructions:

1. In a medium bowl, whisk together the confectioners' sugar, honey, and lavender extract.
2. Mix until the icing is smooth and spreadable.
3. Spread the icing over cooled cookies.
4. Allow the icing to set for at least 15 minutes before serving or storing the cookies.

Blue Cheese and Pear Icing

Ingredients:

- 1 cup confectioners' sugar
- 2 tablespoons melted butter
- 2 ounces crumbled blue cheese
- 1/4 cup diced pear

Instructions:

1. In a medium bowl, whisk together the confectioners' sugar, melted butter, crumbled blue cheese, and diced pear.
2. Mix until the icing is smooth and spreadable.
3. Spread the icing over cooled cookies.
4. Allow the icing to set for at least 15 minutes before serving or storing the cookies.

Spicy Chocolate Icing

Ingredients:

- 1 cup confectioners' sugar
- 2 tablespoons melted butter
- 1/4 cup cocoa powder
- 1/4 teaspoon cayenne pepper

Instructions:

1. In a medium bowl, whisk together the confectioners' sugar, melted butter, cocoa powder, and cayenne pepper.
2. Mix until the icing is smooth and spreadable.
3. Spread the icing over cooled cookies.
4. Allow the icing to set for at least 15 minutes before serving or storing the cookies.

Honey Sriracha Icing

Ingredients:

- 1 cup confectioners' sugar
- 2 tablespoons honey
- 1 teaspoon sriracha sauce

Instructions:

1. In a medium bowl, whisk together the confectioners' sugar, honey, and sriracha sauce.
2. Mix until the icing is smooth and spreadable.
3. Spread the icing over cooled cookies.
4. Allow the icing to set for at least 15 minutes before serving or storing the cookies.

Maple Syrup and Bacon Icing

Ingredients:

- 1 cup confectioners' sugar
- 2 tablespoons maple syrup
- 2 tablespoons cooked, crumbled bacon

Instructions:

1. In a medium bowl, whisk together the confectioners' sugar, maple syrup, and crumbled bacon.
2. Mix until the icing is smooth and spreadable.
3. Spread the icing over cooled cookies.
4. Allow the icing to set for at least 15 minutes before serving or storing the cookies.

Pickle Juice Icing

Ingredients:

- 1 cup confectioners' sugar
- 2 tablespoons melted butter
- 2 tablespoons pickle juice

Instructions:

1. In a medium bowl, whisk together the confectioners' sugar, melted butter, and pickle juice.
2. Mix until the icing is smooth and spreadable.
3. Spread the icing over cooled cookies.
4. Allow the icing to set for at least 15 minutes before serving or storing the cookies.

Curry Icing

Ingredients:

- 1 cup confectioners' sugar
- 2 tablespoons melted butter
- 1 teaspoon curry powder

Instructions:

1. In a medium bowl, whisk together the confectioners' sugar, melted butter, and curry powder.
2. Mix until the icing is smooth and spreadable.
3. Spread the icing over cooled cookies.
4. Allow the icing to set for at least 15 minutes before serving or storing the cookies.

CONCLUSION

Thank you for joining us on this journey through the world of unusual cookie recipes! We hope that you've enjoyed trying out these unique and tasty treats, and that you've gained a bit of inspiration for your own baking adventures. Remember, the world of cookies is vast and varied, and there are always new and exciting flavors to discover. So don't be afraid to experiment and have fun in the kitchen! Happy baking!

Printed in Great Britain
by Amazon

35126028R00053